THEY CAME TO PLAY

THEY CAME TO PLAY

A Photographic History of

Colorado Baseball

by DUANE A. SMITH *&* MARK S. FOSTER

UNIVERSITY PRESS OF COLORADO

Copyright © 1997 by the University Press of Colorado

Published by the University Press of Colorado
P.O. Box 849
Niwot, Colorado 80544
(303) 530-5337

The University Press of Colorado is a cooperative publishing enterprise supported, in part, by Adams State College, Colorado State University, Fort Lewis College, Mesa State College, Metropolitan State College of Denver, University of Colorado, University of Northern Colorado, University of Southern Colorado, and Western State College of Colorado.

The paper used in this publication meets the minimum requirements of the American National Standard for Information Sciences—Permanence of Paper for Printed Library Materials. ANSI Z39.48-1984.

Library of Congress Cataloging-in-Publication Data

Smith, Duane A.
   They came to play : a photographic history of Colorado baseball /
  by Duane A. Smith & Mark S. Foster
    p. cm.
  Includes bibliographical references and index.
  ISBN 0-87081-433-8 (alk. paper)
  1. Baseball--Colorado--History. 2. Baseball--Colorado--History-
-Pictorial works.   I. Foster, Mark S.   II. Title.
  GV863.C6S65 1997
  796.357'64'09788--dc21   96-52683
                                             CIP

10   9   8   7   6   5   4   3   2   1

To Jay Sanford, Frank Haraway,
and the millions of baseball fans of Colorado,
past, present, and future.

CONTENTS

THEY CAME TO PLAY

INTRODUCTION

Joy in Mudville, Denver, and Durango

On a crystal-clear Arizona day in March 1994, baseball reporter Jerome Holtzman reminisced about his thirty-seven years on the beat. A Cactus League game loomed an hour away, and from the home team dugout he spoke of his love for baseball: "I've almost become a protector of baseball. Although baseball needs no protector. I mean, all these sportswriters you know argue about football and other sports, but baseball is the best sport of all. . . . I like it. I like to watch it. Each game is different. If people say to you, well, that it's a dull game, or they have seen a dull game, they just haven't been watching the game. They don't know what's going on."

This Hall of Fame sportswriter could imagine no better job, even if he had been covering the Chicago White Sox and Cubs during some lean years for both teams. "I'm really happiest when I'm at the ballpark, I really am."

Arnie Harris, award-winning WGN television director, watches and works nearly 160 games each year. "I love baseball. I think baseball is really a director's sport because, one, there's so much happening when the ball is in play and, two, conversely, there's so much not happening between pitches. It's really an artistic sport." Baseball, Harris concluded, "is such a unique sport. I think baseball is healthy as hell. They've got problems, sure, the salary thing is going out of sight, but it's not only baseball." Trials and tribulations, joys and successes—baseball has seen them all since the beginning.

To the baseball fan no better sport exists. It has a way of settling into one's life and never leaving. It can be as comfortable as an old glove or as aggravating as a stone in a player's spikes. Joy does not always come to Mudville, as the fans of the immortal Casey found out when he struck out in the ninth inning. The late commissioner of baseball, A. Bartlett Giamatti, remarked: "It breaks your heart. It is designed to break your heart. The game begins in the spring, when everything else begins again, . . . You count on it, rely on it to buffer the passage of time, to keep the memory of sunshine and high skies alive, and then just when the days are all twilight, when you need it most, it stops."

Each game brings new expectations, and many end with heartbreak. Yet from generation to generation the love of the game is passed on to new fans, overcoming ephemeral owners, players, and scandals that temporarily intrude upon the game. It is the one aspect of nineteenth-century life that fans of those days would still recognize and feel comfortable with on the eve of the twenty-first century. The basic game remains the same. Ken Burns, director of a nine-part television series about baseball, has said, "The game offers a precise mirror in which we can see these complicated people who like to call themselves Americans. You can learn about the tension between labor and management, the ever-present question about race; issues about women, popular culture, advertising; about the notion of heroes and villains; what American myth is compared with fact—baseball contains all of them. I began to hear the notes of time and memory, family and home—baseball is about that, too." President Herbert Hoover, in a less poetic manner, simply said, "Next to religion, baseball has furnished a greater impact on American life than any other institution."

Baseball in the past century has become part of the American experience. An urban sport that seems rural, it has mirrored American history and civilization, influencing cities, literature, business, culture, various world affairs, and public life. It can reflect the worst of America, as it did in when closing its doors to African-American players, and the best, as it did in the late 1940s, when it stood in the forefront of integration.

Colorado has been a component of baseball's history from the first game played in Denver, in the 1860s, through decades of town teams, minor league teams, and local Little League teams to today's Colorado Rockies. The state has mirrored baseball on the national scene and over the years has added a few twists of its own. The game came west with the fifty-niners, took root, and prospered in high mountain valleys and prairie pastures. People played the game, fans watched it, towns supported teams, and baseball helped settle and civilize Colorado. W. P. Kinsella summed up what baseball has meant to the country and to Colorado when he wrote in *Shoeless Joe:* "I don't have to tell you that the one constant through all the years has been baseball. America has been erased like a blackboard, only to be rebuilt and then erased again. But baseball has marked time [while] America has rolled by like a procession of steamrollers."

I.
NINETEENTH-CENTURY DAYS

Baseball came to Colorado, Saturday, April 26, 1862, complete with a primitive box score and a *Rocky Mountain News* reporter's analysis of the Denver team captain's strategy: "The positions of some of his men in the first game were not well selected, and to that fact, and very poor batting, may be attributed the great difference in the score [20–7]."

News owner/editor William Byers and others were already calling baseball the "national game" by then. That affirmation aside, the true essence of baseball lay in what it symbolized about America and Americans. Historian and educator Jacques Barzun understood that distinction when he wrote in 1954: "Whoever wants to know the heart and mind of America had better learn baseball, the rules and realities of the game—and do it by watching first some high school or small-town teams."

Small-town baseball and Colorado went together like boys, firecrackers, and the Fourth of July in the nineteenth century. Small towns and large towns followed the game with equal enthusiasm and determination. Community pride and prestige, not to mention the local dollars wagered on the outcome, hung on the execution of a winning hit or a game-saving out.

Baseball mirrored the promise of nineteenth-century Colorado—every game provided a fresh start. Players were rewarded for the feats they accomplished, not for who they were or where they came from. The opportunity for success was equal for all, once they crossed the foul lines; each player's performance and contribution could be measured and recorded. Baseball united diverse and often fragmented groups of newly arrived Coloradans. Immigrants and tenderfoots, with a little help from an old-timer, could watch, enjoy, and judge the game and immediately feel themselves a part of the community. Like Colorado, which seemed to possess unlimited promise, baseball seemed to proffer "an ideal life, refined and condensed and played within the white lines of a diamond." Though born and developed as an urban game, it could be played in a rural setting, serving to bridge the gap between these two worlds.

Baseball came west with the fifty-niners and immediately took root in Denver. As Colorado grew, so did the sport. It was played in mountain valleys and prairie fields, in farm hamlets and booming mining towns, by railroad workers and cowboys off the range, by store clerks and mine managers. Wives, sweethearts, family, and friends came out to cheer. Baseball was, as William Byers wrote in the *Rocky Mountain News* on March 12, 1862, a sign of progress and civilization. "There is no reason why we here out in this 'neck of woods,'. . . should be behind our eastern brethren in anything; much less in athletic sports and games, considering the healthful and invigorating climate." That "invigorating climate" could wreak havoc with spring baseball or summer afternoon games in the mountain communities.

In the heated rivalries of Colorado's transitory, boom-and-bust, dog-eat-dog nineteenth-century urban world, baseball provided the perfect outlet for local chauvinism; victories and defeats were easily defined. As Telluride's *Evening News* told the world on July 21, 1884, "Capt. Crawford of 'Our Boys,' the champion baseballists of the San Juans, says his club is just dying to do up either Rico or Ouray." Teams from farming communities such as Valmont and Kit Carson could challenge Denver on the diamond, if not in the economic or political world, and they might pull off a victory. No matter the outcome, there was always a chance to regroup and try again another day.

Town pride and the need to overcome a deep measure of embarrassment produced Colorado's greatest nineteenth-century team, the 1882 Leadville Blues. Leadville's silver boom had busted. To regain its former prominence, the city undertook to field the strongest nine possible. Town fathers imported a team of professionals from the East and Midwest. Colorado Springs, Longmont, Denver, Buena Vista, and other teams went down to defeat as the Blues marched on to the state championship. Leadville, in the eyes of its own residents, had regained its glory.

By the turn of the century, Colorado baseball had become one of the doors by which Eastern European immigrants could enter mainstream American life. Denver had already gained and lost a minor league team in the Western League, but it remained the center of Colorado semipro and amateur baseball. However, in the sports pages of local newspapers, baseball found itself taking a back seat to the rage of the 1890s, bicycling.

In the outlying communities, town teams still thrived and competed with nearby rivals, particularly on holidays. A special train or cars often carried fans, players, and perhaps a brass band to the game. Quite typically, a dinner or picnic followed before fans returned home. Towns took these games seriously; Silverton went beyond the bounds of good sportsmanship, according to the *Durango Herald* (July 19, 1892), when it imported "the best battery in the state" for a game against Durango's nine. "Durango can afford to lose a game of base ball," the *Herald* scolded, "but Durango cannot afford to win by questionable methods." Silverton, by fair means or foul, won the game.

Colorado baseball was firmly established by 1900. Parks had largely replaced sandlots and fields, players' equipment had improved from earlier days, and the rules had become standardized. Newspapers carried major and minor league standings and featured articles about the sport, and women's teams ("bloomer girls") had made their debut in the central Rockies. What the new century, a hundred seasons long, might bring only whetted the interest of fans and players.

Before passing on to the new century, however, tarry for a moment in the nineteenth century. Look at the heart and soul of our national pastime's people—the fans, umpires, players, managers, and owners who make the game possible.

Georgetown. Courtesy Colorado Historical Society.

Baseball! It came with the 1859 gold rushers and remains one of the few things from that era that still flourishes in Colorado. It has marked the passing of the seasons ever since. As late baseball commissioner Bart Giamatti remarked, "You count on it, rely on it to buffer the passage of time, to keep the memory of sunshine and high skies alive."

Like their counterparts in the eastern United States, Colorado's towns and cities gave birth to local baseball. Urbanization nourished the game throughout the country; then it spread to rural America. From the first Denver teams to the Colorado Rockies, baseball has taken firm root in urban Colorado. Teams have represented such diverse communities as Georgetown, Montrose, and Lime.

Montrose. Courtesy Center of Southwest Studies.

Lime, a Colorado Fuel and Iron town south of Pueblo. Courtesy Colorado Historical Society.

Courtesy Jay Sanford.

Hall of Fame manager Casey Stengel observed, "Now there's three things you can do in a baseball game: you can win or you can lose or it can rain." That was as true for the 1874 Greeley Calamities as for today's Colorado Rockies. This is the earliest known photograph of a Colorado team.

Courtesy Colorado Mountain History Collection, Lake County Public Library, Leadville.

Leadville has a long baseball heritage, including Colorado's best nineteenth-century team, the 1882 Leadville Blues. "You can't win any game unless you're ready to win," states an old baseball axiom; the Blues were ready. No photo of that team exists; this is its 1888 descendant. Note the fancy uniforms and the bat sheaths.

Courtesy National Baseball Hall of Fame.

Dave Foutz, the star player for the 1882 Leadville Blues and the best to take the field in nineteenth-century Colorado. Their best pitcher, "a paralyser and make no mistake," and leading hitter, he later played and managed in the major leagues for St. Louis and Brooklyn from 1884–96, batting .277 (.357 in 1888) and compiling a pitching record of 147–66, including 41 wins in 1886.

Courtesy Maureen Nicholls.

The Fairplay team was in Breckenridge when this photo was taken. Nine players, one mascot, today's batboy, and four nattily dressed men (manager and sponsors?) pose behind the catcher's equipment. "A baseball manager is a necessary evil," observed one of the game's legendary managers, Sparky Anderson.

Courtesy Museum of Western Colorado.

A most dapper team, the Denver & Rio Grande nine out of Grand Junction. Many players may be smoking cigars. Company-sponsored teams were common by the turn of the century. "The only real happiness a ballplayer has is when he is playing a ball game and accomplishes something he didn't think he could do," wrote Ring Lardner, whose celebrated sportswriting career began in Pueblo.

Courtesy Center of Southwest Studies.

Fort Lewis became an Indian boarding school in 1891, and what better way to "walk the white man's road" than to play baseball. The team became one of the best in southwestern Colorado, playing many of the local town teams and more than holding their own.

Courtesy Colorado Historical Society.

The Boston Bloomer Girls played in Denver in 1892; they had a private car for their "Tour Across the Continent." Women's teams started to appear in the 1890s, sometimes with a male battery. Here the pitcher is a woman, the catcher a man. By 1994 Colorado had a professional women's team, the Silver Bullets.

The serious-looking 1889 Silver Plume nine look ready to take on the world. The plaque seems to indicate they won something. As the old baseball saying goes, "When you win, you eat better, sleep better and your beer tastes better."

Courtesy George Hassan.

Two unidentified teams and their fans stand against a mountain backdrop. Too often, baseball overlooks the fans. As Andy McPhail, member of a four-generation baseball family and current president of the Chicago Cubs, observed, "Players come and go, owners come and go, but the game remains, and the fans are what makes the game unique."

Courtesy Maureen Nicholls.

The 1900 Gold Pan Mining Company team stands in front of the company machine shops in Breckenridge. The uniforms are most interesting and appear to be patterned after the players' working clothes. That baseball sage, Yogi Berra, observed, "Uniforms are all the same. Some are just hotter than others."

Courtesy Jay Sanford.

The love of baseball starts with youngsters, even those who—like these Silverton girls in 1884—have to use a boulder for home plate. When asked why he played so hard every game, Joe DiMaggio replied: "Because there is always some kid who may be seeing me for the first or last time. I owe him my best."

Pueblo's batterymates stand side by side in the back row next to their manager in their ballpark. Pueblo has a long baseball heritage of amateur and professional teams.

Courtesy San Juan County Historical Society.

A mining town without a baseball team was a rarity—high elevations and short seasons did not deter the faithful. Slattery's Invincibles, sponsored by necktie-bedecked saloon man and mining investor Jack Slattery, upheld Silverton's honor against other San Juan towns. Drinking and baseball have been around since the first pitch. Casey Stengel remarked, "They say some of my stars drink whiskey, but I have found that the ones who drink milkshakes don't win many ballgames."

Courtesy Jay Sanford.

An Alamosa amateur club poses proudly in 1886. Billy Adams, standing third from left, later became governor of Colorado, 1927–33. Note the size of the bats. Bats have played a large role in baseball superstition. "When I struggle at the plate I ask the trainer for eye drops and put them right on my bat so my bat can see the ball good," remarked one frustrated player.

Courtesy Jay Sanford.

For much of the nineteenth century the national pastime, as practiced in Colorado, was a leisurely activity enjoyed by gentlemen in open fields. This 1889 photo of a contest at Estes Park suggests players more interested in picnics than popups.

Courtesy Jay Sanford.

Lawyers and baseball have not always gotten along well, especially in recent years. A disgusted Bill Veeck sarcastically observed: "Attorneys should wear numbers on their backs, and box scores should have entries for writs, dispositions and appeals." Things appeared more tranquil in 1898, when a University of Denver Law School team posed for a photo.

Courtesy Jay Sanford.

The Old Loveland Grays assume a proud, even defiant, pose for a team photo, circa 1910. "There's sunshine, fresh air, and the team's behind us," declared Hall of Famer Ernie Banks. "Let's play two."

Courtesy Colorado Historical Society.

Baseball is a combination of jans, players, game, and stadium. The setting might be Wrigley Field and its vines, or it might be a mountain glen near Georgetown and Silver Plume. Wrigley Field, sportswriter E. M. Swift said, "is a Peter Pan of a ballpark. It has never grown up, and it has never grown old." This field, however, is now buried under rock and an interstate highway.

Courtesy Gilpin County Historical Society.

Baseball and women had come a long way by the turn-of-century as shown by the fact that Gilpin County fielded two teams (c1905). No doubt old-timers were as shocked by this as women voting and demanding their "rights." The "Miners" are identified, the women are not.

2.
HOMETOWN TEAMS

The years between the turn of the century and the Great Depression found town baseball at its zenith in Colorado. Changing times, fascinating decades—the state and nation went through Theodore Roosevelt, the Progressive Era, the Great War, the Roaring Twenties, and the Crash of 1929. Change could be seen everywhere, nowhere more clearly than with the emergence of new technologies such as the automobile, motion pictures, airplanes, and radio. These would have been wonders to the Coloradan of 1900 but ordinary, everyday things to the Coloradan of 1930. Each of these innovations helped break down the barriers that for so long had shaped Coloradans' lives; together they helped bring the state into mainstream America.

Meanwhile, hard-rock mining declined; no new exciting gold or silver rushes rejuvenated the industry, and an era ended. Coal mining flourished amid labor troubles, but even severe tensions did not prevent the mining companies from fielding local teams. Agriculture on the eastern plains and in the western valleys snatched its moment in the economic sun, then slumped, while industrial Pueblo prospered and tourist traffic shifted from trains to autos. Denver grew as never before and remained Colorado's baseball center.

The national pastime, meanwhile, marked the changing seasons with regularity and assurance, arriving with the coming of warm spring days and drifting away with the yellow aspen of fall. Fortunes in the mining camps and farming villages rose and fell, but baseball was always there to arouse pride and excitement even in the most economically depressed times.

Not that baseball remained static; it did not. Continued improvement of equipment and playing fields, and innovations in strategy inspired by the fame of power-hitting Babe Ruth, transformed it forever. The "inside game" of bunts, singles, and stolen bases that New York Giants manager John McGraw developed and refined at the turn of the century was fine in its day, but the home run enabled teams to snatch victory from defeat with one swing of the bat. What better could describe the American attitude of the 1920s than Ruth and the home run?

The desire of Coloradans to play the national game appeared in a variety of ways. On a "windy and bad day" in June 1908, Alex Botkin and the Tomboy team descended from 11,500-foot Savage Basin to 8,500-foot Telluride for a game. They lost 16–4 on a field that shortstop Botkin described this way in a letter: "[T]he infield was fairly level but the outfield had many tree stumps sticking up."

Far out on the windswept eastern plains, the Lamar Cardinals played the Holly Bloomer Girls in 1906. The report of the game concluded: "The wonderful lady pitcher proved to be Connors of Holly. All the Lamar boys wanted to play infield positions so as to intercept the Bloomer Girls in their attempts to steal bases, and the matter was finally compromised by allowing them to shift positions every inning to give all of them an opportunity to see the girls at close range." They should have paid more attention to the game; Lamar lost, 7–2. Such embarrassments aside, town teams became very popular in northeastern Colorado. Sunday, the farmers' leisure day, featured church and baseball. Colorado plainsmen even organized their own Corn Belt Baseball League, which included clubs from Sterling, Haxtun, Holyoke, Sedgwick, Julesburg, and Fleming.

Superintendent William Peterson at the Fort Lewis Indian School complained that government regulations forced him to purchase "inferior-quality balls" that wore out far too quickly. He informed federal authorities that the team was not "composed of small boys, but young men," aged seventeen and eighteen, who play teams in all the surrounding towns. Despite their substandard equipment, they played the game very well and proved to be highly regarded opponents.

Changing times doomed this baseball era. By the mid-1920s radio and the sports page brought professional baseball to fans, decreasing interest somewhat in the local nines. Other sports, such as football, basketball, golf, and tennis, started to encroach upon baseball's dominance. The automobile tempted both young players and older fans to pursue other leisure interests. Then came the crash and the Great Depression, which closed businesses and bankrupted companies that once had sponsored teams. High schools and colleges were forced to cut back their athletic budgets and programs, and hard economic times made it generally more difficult to field teams. Finally, World War II, the postwar emergence of television, and an amazing variety of new interests and activities for Coloradans spelled the end of town baseball. A few communities continued to field teams, but support never approached what it once had been.

The game persevered; nevertheless, something had been lost at the grassroots level—something that would never be recovered, a memory of a time that once was, a dream of yesterday. The days so cherished by this poem that appeared in Telluride's *San Miguel Examiner* on May 18, 1907 were as gone as that town's mining prominence.

In the spring the young girl's fancy
lightly turns to thoughts of hat,
In the spring the thrifty housewife
washes windows and all that,
In the spring the clothing drummer
lays in new supplies of gall,
In the spring the young man's fancy
lightly turns to thoughts of ball.

Look carefully at the shadows of a vanished America that appear on the following pages. They tell much about a time and a place and even about ourselves. As author George Will pointedly observed, "The day Custer lost at Little Bighorn, the Chicago White Sox beat the Cincinnati Red Legs 3-2, and both teams wore knickers and still do. Baseball has many continuities. No other sport is so steeped in its own traditions."

Courtesy Big Timbers Museum..

The 1903 Lamar Cardinals strike a formidable pose. They or some of their friends lost to the Holly Bloomer Girls. Maybe the boys agreed with Bill Veeck's later comment on women players: "They'll certainly do something for a uniform that a male athlete can't."

Courtesy Ouray County Historical Society.

Montrose defeated Ouray 14–3 this July 4. The *Ouray Herald* consoled its readers that although the game could not be called "creditable," the team was still "weary" from defeating Telluride the day before. Smoky Joe Wood played on the Ouray team as a teenager. Later, when Wood reached the major leagues, Walter Johnson said, "There is no man alive can throw harder than Smoky Joe Wood."

Courtesy Telluride Historical Museum...

Telluride fielded championship teams despite losing to Ouray. These happy players were the 1913 "champions of the Western Slope." Their diamond was carved out of a mountain valley against the backdrop of the mountains that ringed the town. Telluride's mineral production was second only to Cripple Creek's in these prewar years.

Courtesy Museum of Western Colorado.

The Teller Institute Indian nine and their rivals, the Palisade team, have their photograph taken along with fans and a frisky dog before the game. Fans have arrived in wagons and some fancy carriages. "All baseball fans are provincial," observed sportswriter Art Hall. "They don't want the best team to win, they want their team to win."

Courtesy Brian Levine.

"A winter's day" in Union Park in Cripple Creek. The local nine defends the community's honor and hopefully "wins" the bets placed on the outcome. It was hard to keep fans from betting on the hometown nine; wagering offered too much fun and added a personal excitement to the game.

Courtesy Denver Public Library, Western History Collection.

"This is a game—because it has no clock—which could go on forever. This is a game where its best players fail seven times out of ten—very much like life." Author/producer Ken Burns was right on both counts. Yet this turn-of-the-century La Junta team looks determined to prove him wrong.

At the peak of the district's tungsten boom in 1916, the Nederland team lines up in front of the wire backstop. Wanting to field the best nine possible, local supporters had recruited several of these players to strengthen their team, a common occurrence.

The Liberty Bell Mine (near Telluride) developed into one of Colorado's great producers. Its team, however, seems to be a hodgepodge of uniforms, caps, and gloves. These players probably were actual employees at the mine and smelter, not hired guns brought in to promote the corporate image.

Courtesy Amon Carter Museum, Mazzulla Collection.

"It ain't over till it's over," observed that baseball sage Yogi Berra, and the fans at this Crested Butte game never gave up on their team. Their rivals and fans arrived on the special railroad car parked in the rear, behind the automobiles that finally "did the railroad in."

Courtesy Jack Smith.

The Trinidad players and a second team march in an unidentified parade. Young fans get as close to their heroes as they can, while a band plays at the right. Players had to get used to jeers and cheers and take them all in stride. As the saying goes, "Fans don't boo nobodies."

The farming and ranching town of Collbran in Mesa County fielded a well-dressed nine. Just like their mining contemporaries, they wanted to be the regional best; that reputation helped promote the community in an age that paid heed to the "grow or die" philosophy.

Courtesy Jack Smith.

Look carefully at this pre–World War I Cokedale team. Its players reflect the ethnic character of the coal communities, which differed from that of Collbran. They played teams from nearby coal towns. Cokedale (Fremont County) produced coal and, later, gypsum for the regional economy; its coke ovens supplied coke for Colorado smelters.

Baseball caught the fancy of young and old alike. Long before a Little League team ever took the field, this nine represented the San Luis School, Colorado Springs. Hall of Fame pitcher Bob Lemon threw a strike when he said, "Baseball was made for kids, and grownups only screw it up."

Fans crowd the field on a summer's day as the Marvel–Red Mesa boys take on the Trimble Springs nine. They played the game near the site of Fort Lewis, once a military base, then an Indian school, now, in the 1920s, a rural high school. The straw-hatted umpire stands behind second base. The rocks in the outfield and foul territory must have made fielding difficult.

Photography had improved by the 1920s, particularly with faster camera speed and better film. This action shot was probably taken at Salida or Gunnison; the field sat in the infield of a racetrack. It hardly mattered where the field was; if you built it, the fans would come. And they did, to diamonds scattered throughout the state.

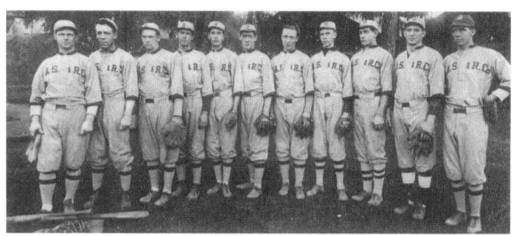

Courtesy Center of Southwest Studies.

The American Smelting and Refining Company team was typical of the corporate-sponsored teams that replaced town teams in some communities. Most of these men probably held some job in Durango's smelter and played baseball on the weekends. Durango's famous newspaperman and poet Dave Day wrote: "The umpire loudly shouts, 'Play Ball'/The players step in view;/The crowd in answer to the call,/Exclaims 'We hope they do.' "

Courtesy La Plata County Historical Society..

The contrast between the AS&RCO nine's uniforms and equipment and those of nearby Ignacio's team is marked. This tri-ethnic community's makeup is clearly represented in the players; uniforms give no indication which team might have been better, although in 1916 Ignacio ended up last in a four-team league that included Bayfield and Pagosa Springs.

Courtesy Pueblo Library District.

Las Animas's Asahi baseball team gave these Japanese Americans an opportunity to compete evenly with their neighbors. Many ethnic teams played in the region from Greeley to Trinidad, as baseball offered them a door to mainstream America. As Ted Williams commented: "Baseball gives every American boy a chance to excel. Not just to be as good as someone else, but to be better. That is the nature of man and the name of the game."

Courtesy La Plata County Historical Society.

Safe! Durango's baseball field was at the fairgrounds. Beyond third base stand both carriages and a car—the past and the future. Baseball is a game of inches complemented by strength and speed; a little daring helps as well. The old motto is true: "You can't steal second with your foot on first."

Courtesy George Hassan.

These unidentified players look determined, if attired in somewhat unusual uniforms. They probably had the same zeal and enthusiasm that Colorado Rockies' manager Don Baylor did in 1995 when reviewing his thirty-year career: "It's covered a lot of ups and downs in this game; I've made a lot of great friendships, and I'm still around, enjoying it the same way I did on the first day I stepped on the field."

Courtesy La Plata County Historical Society.

Baseball, Bart Giamatti wrote, "breaks your heart." He was talking about the seasons, but baseball really breaks fans' hearts because it is about losing. Giamatti was right; only one team eventually triumphs. Whether these Durango fans went home happy or not has been lost to history. Two of the community's three streetcars sit behind the covered grandstand.

Courtesy Jay Sanford.

Bayly Underhill was but one of dozens of companies that sponsored teams in the early twentieth century. Here, both the boys' and girls' teams pose about 1910.

Courtesy Jay Sanford.

The Denver Tramway players pose with their bats crossed in front of them in a rustic setting around 1910. Bats have become part of baseball's mystique. "I used five different bats," said Jose Canseco after going 0-for-5. "I asked, 'Which one of you wants to get a hit?' And they all said, 'Not me.'"

Courtesy Jay Sanford.

Coors Brewery sponsored numerous top-notch semipro clubs in the 1930s and 1940s. Here, several stars from the 1938 team inspect baseballs before a contest at Elitch's Garden.

Courtesy Jay Sanford.

Elitch's hosted semipro and amateur games for many years. Pictured here is a close play at the plate in a 1949 high school contest. We can only hope the umpire—the "villain" of baseball—called this one right. Longtime umpire Beans Reardon had this to say about his profession: "Who can the managers blame losses on? Who can pitchers and hitters blame their troubles on? Believe me, the umpire will always be with us."

Courtesy Jay Sanford.

As the umpire watches, Dick Hotton of the Coors Brewers scores on an inside-the-park home run at Merchants Park in 1940. A traditional umpire's lament says it all: "Umpiring is the only profession where you have to be perfect when you start, then continue to improve."

Courtesy Jay Sanford.

During World War II many future major leaguers played for military and civilian teams in Denver's Victory League. Al Zarilla, far right, is shown in this 1942 photo. He enjoyed considerable success as an outfielder for the St. Louis Browns, Boston Red Sox, and Chicago White Sox, compiling a lifetime batting average of .276 in ten big league seasons.

3.
BLACK BASEBALL IN COLORADO

When contemporary Coloradans think about African Americans' participation in baseball, they most likely consider the achievements of popular Rockies players such as Ellis Burks and Eric Young. Fans with slightly longer memories fondly recall the Triple-A Denver Bears of the late 1970s and early 1980s, when future major league stars, including Ellis Valentine, Andre Dawson, and Tim Raines, terrified opposing hurlers. A few old-timers may remember the first blacks to join the Bears, back in 1951—Curt Roberts and Bill Bruton. The fact that the Class-A Western League club integrated relatively late, five years after the Montreal Royals signed Jackie Robinson, gives little hint of the rich tradition of minority participation in baseball in the region.

Contrary to the popular view that Jackie Robinson was the first black to play in the major leagues, several dozen blacks appeared in at least one game in the 1870s and 1880s. Though by no means a baseball utopia for blacks, Colorado routinely offered skilled players opportunities long after they had been banned by professional leagues elsewhere in the nation. Organized black baseball teams visited Colorado at least as early as 1882. During 1885, the first season of professional baseball in Colorado (in the short-lived Rocky Mountain League), several blacks appeared in uniform for both the Denver and Pueblo clubs. By the 1890s Jim Crow laws banned African Americans from formerly integrated teams. Much to his credit, George Tebeau, owner of the Denver franchise in the Western League, was one of the last owners to hire blacks.

The first three decades of the twentieth century brought little integration in organized and semipro baseball in Colorado, although ambitious sponsors and managers tried occasionally to pass off light-skinned blacks as Native Americans or Cubans. Nevertheless, black baseball thrived in the region. At the turn of the century, several teams vied for recognition as the top black club. In the 1890s the Black Diamonds and Colorado Champions battled for that honor. In the early 1900s the Lipton Teas dominated. The state never had an all-black Negro league as such, but many semipro clubs played for a few seasons, then disappeared. Numerous contests pitting black teams against white clubs took place, but local papers seldom considered interracial competition newsworthy. An exception occurred when one of the premier teams in the Negro League, the Kansas City Monarchs, visited Denver in 1922 to play a five-game set against the Denver Bears.

Although challenged occasionally by the Goalstone Brothers and the Denver Monarchs, the most established black club in Denver was the White Elephants, which played between 1915 and 1935. Sponsored by local black businessman A.H.W. Ross, the White Elephants featured numerous stars who played for many years. Perhaps the two most notable players were infielder Theodore "Bubbles" Anderson and a fireballing right-handed pitcher named Tom "Pistol Pete" Albright. Anderson, Albright, and several other members of the club played in the Negro League, but most disliked the constant travel and eventually returned to the White Elephants.

Colorado was by no means a mecca for racial tolerance, having been dominated politically by the Ku Klux Klan in the early to mid-1920s. Contests between white and black teams were sometimes marred by ugly brawls and beaning incidents. Nevertheless, the state had been one of the last to segregate baseball, and it was one of the first to challenge that practice.

Local baseball promoters had organized the *Denver Post* tournament in 1915, an annual semi-pro event extending over a full week that attracted mostly regional teams for its first few years. In 1934 *Post* sports editor Charles Lyman "Poss" Parsons invited the Kansas City Monarchs to appear in the tournament. Attracted by a jackpot of roughly $5,000, big money in the Depression, the Missourians accepted. Parsons counted on the Monarchs to contend for the crown against the House of David team, which represented a Michigan-based religious order. The latter club was notable partly because almost all of its players sported both long hair and extraordinary beards. Although the House of David sect did not admit blacks, its baseball team hired the renowned black hurler Satchel Paige. Paige was well known in the black community but was not yet a national figure. However, an important integrated national tournament was big news in 1934. Paige pitched brilliantly and attracted considerable national attention.

Two years later the two clubs garnering the most attention in the *Post* tournament were the House of David team and the Negro National League All-Stars. The latter, with members from the Homestead Grays, Pittsburgh Crawfords, and Washington, D.C., Elite Giants featured many of the legendary players of the period, virtually a "Who's Who" of black baseball. Four future Hall of Fame members appeared: Paige, catcher Josh Gibson, outfielder Cool Papa Bell, and first baseman Buck Leonard. Historian Jay Sanford, an expert on black baseball, argues that the 1936 tournament boasted the strongest group of teams ever fielded. Nevertheless, the black easterners easily swept through the early rounds. In the finale, the All-Stars shut out Enid, Oklahoma's Eason Oilers 7–0, as Paige whiffed eighteen batters. Fans of both races thronged to Merchants Park, home of the Denver Bears, located on Broadway just south of the former Montgomery Ward building. About 11,000 squeezed their way into the rickety ballpark, and hundreds had to be turned away at the gate. Like most other fans, renowned *Post* sportswriter Leonard Cahn was awed by the performance of the All-Stars: "It has been many a year since Denver has seen the likes of them. They're the cream in your coffee, the icing on your cake, the champagne in your cocktail. They're class."

No other black team made quite such a splash at the *Denver Post* tournament, but the Ciudad Trujillo team, invited to the affair in 1937, came close. In order to improve chances for his favorite team, Santo Domingo dictator Rafael Trujillo, a rabid baseball fan, had hired a number of Negro League players at generous salaries. Inspired perhaps by heavily armed guards, the Americans performed well under intense pressure and won the Dominican League's championship. Their midsummer visit to Denver was, by contrast, a pleasant interlude. The Trujillo All-Stars won their first six games, allowing a total of four runs to their opponents. Some internal dissension then emerged. The winning pitcher in the championship game would earn a $1,000 bonus, and the All-Stars wanted it to go to Leroy Matlock, who had been with the team for some months. But promoters had insisted that Paige should be the starter. According to one participant, recounting the story fifty years later, the All-Stars intentionally threw their next game, losing 6–4 to Halliburton Cement. Since both teams now owned 6–1 records, they would meet in the championship game. Matters were straightened out between the All-Stars and the promoters. Matlock pitched the All-Stars to an 11–1 victory in the title game and was awarded the bonus.

The 1937 tournament was marred by a vicious brawl in an early-round game between the All-Stars and the Pampa (Texas) Oilers. The Oilers featured third baseman Sammy Hale, formerly of the Philadelphia Athletics, and Portland, Oregon, pitcher Dan Mills. These two players, accustomed to segregated baseball, apparently baited their opponents. The Trujillo club was used to competing in front of unfriendly crowds and would not be intimidated by anybody. Early in the game there were several rough collisions, causing outbreaks of temper. Later, Cool Papa Bell spiked Hale while running out an extra-base hit, and a fight broke out. The ugliness quickly escalated, and players from both clubs grabbed bats and started swinging. Four All-Stars were ejected, but no white players were dismissed.

Perhaps because of this incident, no black teams appeared in the 1938 tournament. The next year, however, the Ethiopian Clowns were invited. The Clowns were a baseball version of basketball's Harlem Globetrotters. They came to play with bare feet and wearing grass skirts; in addition, they sported African-sounding names. They were talented but not at the level of earlier black all-star aggregations. The Clowns were eliminated by the eventual champions, the Eason Oilers. In 1940 they returned and eliminated Coors Brewery's excellent club but were knocked off themselves by a team from Mount Pleasant, Texas. Persistence finally paid off in 1941 when the Clowns emerged victorious. In the final, they defeated the previous year's champion, Bona-Allen of Georgia, by a 9–7 score. The losing pitcher was Sig Jakucki, who would later star for the St. Louis Browns when they won their only pennant, in 1944.

The *Denver Post* tournament was suspended during the war years, when Victory League teams representing nearby military bases dominated the regional semi-pro scene. After the war, the *Post* tournament was revived for just two years, 1946 and 1947. In the final year, blacks were represented by the Cincinnati Crescents, a traveling team featuring Cool Papa Bell. They were good enough to reach the finals. However, the Coors Brewers routed them in the championship game, 19–6.

Nevertheless, black teams and players starred in many of the region's most important baseball exhibitions between the 1880s and the late 1940s. With the revival of the Class-A Western League Denver Bears in 1947, semi-pro baseball quickly faded. Organized baseball was already integrated, albeit on a small scale. In subsequent decades, more and more African Americans would wear the crisp uniforms of white professional clubs. By the mid-1950s Negro League teams were selling most of their stars to major league teams, and the league soon folded. By mid-century, the presence of blacks on almost all baseball diamonds was an established (if not universally accepted) fact. Colorado had played a key role in creating such long-delayed progress.

Hispanics sponsored teams of their own. Rudy Peralta, superintendent for the Great Western Sugar Company in Greeley, sponsored the team bearing his name for many years. This photo was taken around 1910.

Courtesy Emi Chikuma, Brighton..

Japanese Americans in Colorado adopted the national pastime with enthusiasm. Here is the S Ban Company (importers) of Denver team in the 1920s.

Courtesy Emi Chikuma, Brighton.

Before the tensions between Japanese Americans and other Americans intensified following Pearl Harbor, most amateur teams were still segregated by race. Here, a group of amateur Japanese American ballplayers from Ft. Lupton pose proudly, about 1939 or 1940.

Courtesy Jay Sanford.

A Japanese American doctor sponsored a club under his name in Denver during the 1920s. The Kunitomos, with white and Japanese American players, lasted about a decade.

Courtesy Jay Sanford.

African Americans played on integrated teams in the region well into the 1890s, but baseball was segregated by early in the twentieth century. By the end of the 1920s, numerous black clubs had won local fame. Perhaps the best was the Denver White Elephants, posed here in 1930. Star pitcher Tom "Pistol Pete" Albright (back row, center) once struck out 23 batters in a Merchants Park game in 1933.

Courtesy Jay Sanford.

Oliver "Ollie the Ghost" Marcelle, a third baseman with the Kansas City Monarchs, had catlike reflexes and was considered the Negro Leagues' best at the position. He arranged to bring the Monarchs to the *Denver Post* tournament in 1934, integrating the event for the first time. He is buried in Denver at the Fairmount Mortuary.

Courtesy Jay Sanford.

The 1934 Kansas City Monarchs, runners-up in the *Denver Post* tournament that year. Ironically, they lost out to a predominantly white club, the House of Davids, whose pitching staff was anchored that year by legendary black hurler Satchel Paige.

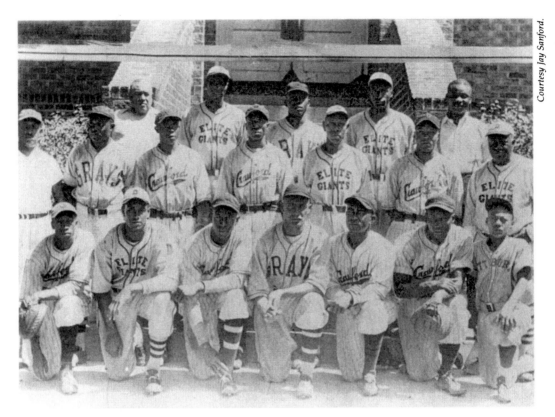

Courtesy Jay Sanford.

The Negro National League All-Stars, winners of the 1936 *Denver Post* tournament. This team featured several legendary black stars, including Satchel Paige (front row, third from left), Josh Gibson (front row, second from right) and Cool Papa Bell (middle row, center).

4.
MINOR LEAGUE BASEBALL

Back in the 1870s, *Rocky Mountain News* editor William Byers had refused to carry news about baseball because he detested the "unwholesome" influence of gamblers and paid professionals on what formerly had been an innocent form of recreation for youths and "gentlemen." By the early twentieth century, however, baseball fans had long since become accustomed to the idea of grown men who earned a living by striving to win contests by any means, fair or foul. Many fathers urged their sons to emulate star New York Giants hurler Christy Mathewson, noted for his gentlemanly deportment and good sportsmanship, but most fans urged their hometown heroes to imitate the hell-bent-for-leather, win-at-all-costs tactics of John "Mugsy" McGraw or Ty Cobb.

From the beginning, the professional game exerted a magnetic pull on the youth of America. When writing autobiographies, countless successful men recalled that their first major disappointment in life was the realization that they lacked the skills to play the game at the professional level. Why did baseball evoke such a passionate response? A century ago, few professional players achieved economic security from baseball alone. After a spectacular play, fans might shower the field with coins, which, by custom, went into the pocket of the player responsible for the outpouring of appreciation, but such occurrences were not that common. A star player even at the major league level earned only enough to support a family in modest comfort, with maximum salaries at about $2,500 per year as late as 1900. At the minor league level, most players had to scuffle to make ends meet. Hardly anybody got rich playing the game.

The earliest professional Denver nines were composed of men who worked hard during the off-season as cowboys, farmers, miners, clerks, blacksmiths, and bakers. But during the baseball season, young boys considered these hometown players gods. What lad ever forgot that first summer afternoon when his father took him to the local park to see graceful giants in dazzling uniforms, fielding and throwing with stunning skill and hitting with awesome power? Even if a father reminded his son that few of the players were gentlemen, smart boys realized that the men on the field got to leave the boring routine of the workaday world to play a wondrous game five months of the year. And what youngster would not long to be wearing a uniform, sitting in an open-air touring car, waving to people lining the streets at an opening day parade through downtown Denver? Or any other city in America, for that matter.

Few contemporary Coloradans can remember when baseball was the only professional team sport in the state, but such was the case for many decades. Professional ball made its first noticeable appearance in Colorado a full mile above Denver, in Leadville, "the city in the clouds." During the 1882 season the Leadville Blues fielded a juggernaut, even featuring some men who had played at the major league level. The first avowedly professional nine from Denver competed against the Leadville Blues and the Pueblo Pastimes in 1885 in the so-called Rocky Mountain League, but ambitious regional promoters longed for recognition in larger circles. Pueblo also fielded teams intermittently in various short-lived minor leagues. Joining the Western League as a charter member in 1886, the Denver club competed against teams from Omaha, Topeka, and other plains cities. To the joy of local fans, Denver won the first official Western League pennant.

However, minor league baseball in Colorado and Denver hardly experienced uninterrupted success. Although baseball was the only regularly scheduled "play-for-pay" game in town until the arrival of the Denver Broncos in 1960, many other forms of entertainment competed for residents' disposable income. This competition persisted throughout Denver's years as a minor league baseball city. Almost from its founding, Denver promoted its healthful climate and its reputation as a vacation mecca. Many visitors spent leisurely days in the mountains rather than at the ballpark. Locals were often diverted by active outdoor recreation, beginning with the bicycle craze in the late 1880s. In the 1890s the nation experienced a severe national depression, which hit Colorado particularly hard. Local citizens had little money to spend on necessities, let alone admissions to professional baseball games. As a consequence, promoters fielded professional teams on an extremely sporadic basis in that decade.

Early in the new century, automobile touring, picnicking, hiking, backpacking, and camping became favored activities during the baseball season. Later, sedentary diversions such as radio, movies, television, and video games kept Coloradans away from the ballparks.

Nevertheless, between the appearance of the Leadville Blues in 1882 and the departure of the Denver Zephyrs 111 years later, diehard fans in Colorado were treated to some of the best minor league baseball in the country; and the Colorado Springs Sky Sox, the Colorado Rockies' top farm club, continues to draw thousands of enthusiastic followers. During many years, Denver, Pueblo, and Colorado Springs all fielded teams in one professional league or another. Old-timers remember the thrill of rooting against teams from other Colorado cities when league pennants were at stake. If one town's team was hopelessly out of the chase, its faithful followers still delighted in deflating the hopes of an in-state rival. Carloads of Pueblo fans might take long weekend trips to Denver to root for their beloved Dodgers against the big, bad Denver Bears. Over more than a century of organized baseball in Colorado, the professional game assumed a distinct regional character.

The number of Colorado hurlers who have gone on to successful major league careers is rather small. Modern fans might point with pride to regional products such as Rich "Goose" Gossage, Omar "Turk" Lown, and Brian Fisher; others, such as Hubert "Dutch" Leonard and Jeff Pfeffer, labored briefly for the Denver Bears on their way up to the big leagues. However, even the most skilled local hurlers seldom advanced beyond the minor leagues. Such storied pitchers as Caveman Greer and Hippo Hodges, for example, toiled successfully year after year in Bears uniforms in the 1920s and 1930s but never made it to the big leagues. While a number of skilled batsmen tore the cover off the ball in the state's mile-high altitude, most failed in brief trials at the major league level.

Even in the old days, baseball men realized that curveballs didn't react so well at high altitude and that batted balls traveled farther in thin air than they would at sea level. At the close of the twentieth century, these truths still dominate. In the many decades during which pitching statistics have been kept, no Denver pitching staff has ever led its league in team earned run average. Crafty pitchers learned not to be too upset about yielding homers in Denver. Some, like Bryn Smith, used their experience to good advantage. After compiling a 15–5 record for the Denver Bears in 1981, Smith won promotion to the Montreal Expos. Twelve years later, with his successful major league career winding down, he signed with the fledgling Colorado Rockies. Used to pressure and to pitching at altitude, Smith enjoyed one of his greatest moments of glory as the Rockies' starting pitcher on April 9, 1993 in the first regular-season major league game ever played in the state of Colorado. Smith tossed seven shutout innings against the Montreal Expos to earn the victory, the Rockies' first-ever regular-season triumph, in front of more than 80,000 ecstatic fans.

Colorado has always been a haven for sluggers; it was a rare Denver Bears team that did not boast them in numbers. A few brawny batsmen, including Andre Dawson, Ellis Valentine, Greg Vaughn, Bill "Moose" Skowron, Tim Wallach, Warren Cromartie, and Jeff Burroughs, went on to enjoy varying degrees of success at the major league level. But some fabled sluggers at high altitude were ordinary at sea level. In the 1980s Randy Bass put up monster numbers at Mile High Stadium (Bears Stadium for purists). Though he enjoyed some success playing in Japan, Bass's post-Bears career was basically disappointing. The same held true for "Marvelous" Marv Throneberry, a prodigious slugger for the Bears during the "Yankees years" of the late 1950s. Some considered him the next Babe Ruth. Perhaps his legendary ineptitude with the glove broke his confidence. Maybe Casey Stengel's meandering anecdotes distracted him, or perhaps the pressure to become the hapless New York Mets' chief run producer in the early 1960s sapped his spirit. Throneberry was truly marvelous in Denver, but he flopped in the Big Apple.

Over more than a century of good years and bad, triumphs and disappointments, Colorado's minor leaguers kept the spirit of baseball alive and well in the Rocky Mountain region. When the greatest day in the state's baseball history dawned on April 9, 1993, Coloradans were ready to prove that they were the nation's most numerous, if not the most knowledgeable, fans. Deep knowledge is often accompanied by cynicism, and this generation's major leaguers on the Colorado Rockies' roster have been blessed with almost entirely uncritical adulation. How long the honeymoon between players and fans will last is anyone's guess, but the former hope it will last forever.

Courtesy Jay Sanford.

Professional baseball has been played in Colorado for more than a century. The Colorado Springs Reds, members of the loosely organized state league in 1882. Two players, Ed Kent (standing, far right) and Bill Traffley (seated, center), also played in the major leagues.

Courtesy Jay Sanford.

George "White Wings" Tebeau was a nationally renowned baseball man who almost single-handedly kept the professional game alive in Denver. He played major league ball for several clubs, owned several minor league franchises, and co-founded the American League with sportswriter Byron "Ban" Johnson. Denver was his first love; he built Broadway Park and for many years promoted the Denver Bears and semi-pro baseball.

Courtesy Jay Sanford.

COPYRIGHTED 1888 BY
GOODWIN & CO. N.Y.

OLIVER TEBBAU B. CLEVELAND

Oliver W. "Patsy" Tebeau, George's brother, played briefly for Denver in 1887, then went on to a distinguished career in the major leagues as an infielder and manager. His lifetime batting average over thirteen seasons was .280. As a manager for ten-plus seasons, he never led a pennant winner, but his teams had a combined winning percentage of .560.

Courtesy Jay Sanford.

This is the earliest known photo of Joe Tinker, posed here as a nineteen-year-old infielder for the 1900 Denver club. A bit raw as a youngster, he was eventually cut by Denver, but he went on to fame as part of the Chicago Cubs' storied "Tinker-to-Evers-to-Chance" infield. He is a member of the Baseball Hall of Fame.

When professional baseball returned to Denver in 1900, spring training was casual and informal. Here, two dozen hopefuls in a ragtag collection of uniforms from previous teams pose at Broadway Park a few days before the opening game.

Courtesy Jay Sanford.

Denver's entry in the Western League would go on to win the league pennant in 1900, although few would have predicted such a miracle when this opening day photo was taken. The shed in dead center field is the clubhouse. The large flag flowing in the brisk wind is Denver's 1886 pennant.

Courtesy Jay Sanford.

The 1900 Denver Bears, on their way to the Western League pennant, pose for this team photo at Broadway Park midway through the season.

Courtesy Denver Public Library, Western History Collection.

Ballplayers and team personnel at the turn of the century did not always set sterling examples of clean living as the obviously posed scene at Denver's Broadway Park in 1900 clearly suggests.

Denver's 1900 pennant-winning club poses in front of an advertising billboard in center field at Broadway Park. Note the disparity in uniforms, especially jerseys and hats. Presumably, their attire was more effectively coordinated when they were playing regular-season games.

Courtesy Jay Sanford.

After a decade-long drought, the Denver Bears would win three straight Western League crowns (1911–13) under fiery manager Jack Hendricks. Here is the 1911 club. Note the small mascot in the second row, right.

Courtesy Jay Sanford.

Scene from Broadway Park, looking toward home plate from the third base stands. The seats were packed on this occasion, perhaps for a Bears doubleheader on a Sunday afternoon. The stadium was located on the west side of Broadway at Sixth Avenue.

The 1904 Colorado Springs Millionaires, fierce rivals of the Denver Bears. Note the "$" logo on the jerseys. The nickname derived from the city's reputation as a health spa and resort for rich easterners.

Opening day 1923 at Merchants Park. Bears owner Milton Anfinger leads the team mascot. The team is lined up, with the visiting "Omahogs" from Omaha behind them. Note the automobiles lined up down the left field foul line.

Anfinger receives wreaths on opening day 1923 at Merchants Park. The tokens of fortune did little good, as the club struggled to a 59–107 mark in the Western League.

The 1923 Denver Bears appeared formidable in a team photo but finished last in the Western League. The Bears never won a pennant during the "Roaring Twenties" but they usually finished near the top of the Western League standings.

In the late 1940s and early 1950s, Western League clubs in Colorado Springs and Pueblo regularly challenged the Denver Bears for league titles. This is the 1953 Colorado Springs club.

Courtesy F. Haraway.

During the Bears' successful 1953 Western League pennant drive, the club enjoys a break from the pressure of the campaign.

Courtesy F. Haraway.

Joe Caffie of the Indianapolis Indians steps into the box as the first batter ever to appear in a Triple-A game in Denver, in 1955. Also pictured are catcher Darrell Johnson and umpire John Mullen.

The mid-1950s marked the heyday of the Bears' "Yankee years." Here, future major leaguers Marv Throneberry, Ryne Duren, and Norm Seibern trade barbs.

Courtesy F. Haraway.

In this 1957 American Association game, Wichita manager Ben Geraghty and Harry Hanebrink chew out umpire Dave Carabba.

Courtesy F. Haraway.

The 1992 Denver Zephyrs, Denver's last minor league team. Many die-hard baseball fans lamented the decision to change the team's name from the Bears to the Zephyrs. During the club's last few years in Denver, attendance slowly fell off, and few cared when it moved to New Orleans.

5.

MAJOR LEAGUE BASEBALL

April 9, 1993, marked one of the most significant dates in the history of Colorado. At 3:06 P.M., veteran pitcher Bryn Smith hurled a slider toward Montreal Expos leadoff hitter Mike Lansing, who took the pitch for a ball. After decades of waiting and hoping, of seemingly encouraging developments followed by crushing disappointments, Coloradans finally had major league baseball. This was no mere exhibition game between barnstorming teams. It was a real game that counted in the National League standings.

On that magical, balmy April afternoon, the newborn Colorado Rockies thrashed the Expos 11–4, the first regular season victory in franchise history after two losses in New York to open the season. The victory appeared preordained the moment second baseman Eric Young, the very first Rockies hitter to make a plate appearance before the home folks, blasted a home run. Exactly 80, 227 fans witnessed that historic game in person at Mile High Stadium.

In future years, no doubt millions will claim to have been in attendance that day. If so, perhaps they can be forgiven, as many millions of Coloradans and out-of-state visitors did watch the Rockies play during their inaugural season. In fact, the Rockies set major league attendance records beginning with the first home game. The opening crowd set an all-time record for attendance at a single game. For the season, the team broke virtually every important attendance record, including total tickets sold: 4,483,350. The *smallest* crowd for any game that opening season exceeded 45,000 for a midweek afternoon game against the other expansion team, the Florida Marlins. The level of support stunned even the most optimistic members of the Rockies' front office.

In retrospect, the rousing welcome for major league baseball should perhaps not have come as a surprise. Denver had always enjoyed a reputation for being a great football town, providing devoted support for the Broncos in good years and bad. But the Queen City had usually been a good baseball town too. The minor league Denver Bears had a storied past and set minor league attendance records of their own during the early 1980s.

Few of the wildly enthusiastic fans who departed Mile High Stadium after the Rockies' initial victory realized the full extent of the agonizing struggle to bring major league baseball to Colorado. Many natives of Denver recalled how hopes were raised, then dashed back in the 1970s, when it appeared that oil magnate Marvin Davis had made a deal to purchase the Oakland Athletics from Charles O. Finley and move the club to Denver. In all likelihood, even fewer spectators realized that the south stands, long the home of perhaps the most dedicated and vocal Broncos fans, had originally been built in the expectation that major league baseball would come to Colorado in the early 1960s.

Amazingly, Denver's flirtation with major league baseball has even deeper roots, going back more than a century. In 1887 the local pro team was in only its second season in the Western League, but a few baseball promoters actually talked of bringing a major league franchise to Denver. A century ago professional baseball was remarkably unstable, and there was no clear-cut definition of "major league." In the 1880s and early 1890s, both the Union Association and the Players' League billed themselves as major leagues. The American Association made similar claims. During the 1887 season, Denver interests investigated the possibility of moving the American Association's St. Louis franchise to Denver. In fact, the *Rocky Mountain News* announced on July 25 that the St. Louis Browns were moving out. Although nothing came of the rumors, a seed had been planted.

For the next four decades there was little or no talk of major league baseball's coming to Colorado. In fact, promoters had enough difficulty maintaining minor league baseball, and the Denver Bears experienced more bad years than prosperous ones. However, when the Bears won three consecutive Western League pennants between 1911 and 1913, attendance was excellent, and fan enthusiasm appeared high. Unfortunately, major league baseball was in disarray. The National League and the American League had reached an understanding in 1901. But deep fissures weakened the agreement, and the precarious peace was too fragile to last. Rival entrepreneurs and renegade ballplayers, the latter upset over low salaries and poor working conditions, established the Federal League in 1914. The new league lasted only two years, but it symbolized the hopes and frustrations of promoters and cities that were excluded from the major leagues. During the years surrounding World War I, some boosters of the national game envisioned elevating several established loops—including the International League, the Pacific Coast League, and even the Western League—into "major" leagues. In the spring of 1915, Denver newspapers were full of rumors that a higher brand of baseball would soon arrive in the Mile High City, but once again such talk was no more than hot air. Even worse, during World War I interest in the minor league Denver Bears dwindled, and the team's owners were forced to suspend operations for several years.

The Bears fielded teams intermittently between the two world wars. After their revival in 1947 they played in Denver continuously, being renamed the Zephyrs in 1985 and finally yielding the diamond to the Rockies. Four decades ago, promotion to a higher minor-league classification was cause for celebration. In the mid-1950s civic leaders in Denver considered the Queen City deserving of better baseball than that played in the Class-A Western League and lobbied successfully for the Bears' promotion to the Triple-A American Association. This reclassification occurred in 1955, which meant that players in Denver uniforms were only one step away from the majors. Still, the Bears experienced some lean years, particularly after television coverage of major league games began competing for fans' attention. During the 1960s the franchise was forced to seek affiliation with the Pacific Coast League, an unnatural alignment that further eroded support. The club eventually returned to the American Association and by the early 1980s was drawing more than 500,000 spectators each year.

By the late 1970s Denver was a far different city than it had been at the end of World War II. No longer an "overgrown cow town," the city was in the midst of a spectacular economic boom fed by an unprecedented surge in energy development, huge defense contracts, and the rapid growth of firms marketing advanced technologies. In the minds of many civic leaders, sportswriters, and ordinary fans, Denver was a big-league city. Minor league baseball would no longer do.

The most recent flirtation with major league baseball had been in June, 1960, when local newspapers had reported that Denver would field a team in Branch Rickey's proposed new Continental League. Robert Howsam, at the time one of the Bears' owners, had even gone deeply into debt to build the south stands in order to meet the proposed league's minimum seating capacity. But major league owners quietly sabotaged the fledgling organization by buying off the strongest of its financial consortiums and awarding the group a new franchise in the National League, the New York Mets. Howsam was left with unfilled seats in the south stands, and he eventually had to sell his professional sports interests to Denver contractor Gerald H. Phipps.

But in the mid-to-late 1970s, Denver was blessed with wealthy movers and shakers who were determined to bag the elusive prize of a major league team. Few appeared better positioned for the campaign than billionaire oilman Marvin Davis. In late 1977 wire service stories claimed that Davis had completed a deal with Oakland Athletics owner Charles O. Finley to purchase the franchise and move it to Denver. The story was largely true, but "minor complications" remained to be ironed out. As so often happens, loose ends killed the deal, but reports of an impending sale of the franchise repeatedly surfaced during the next few years. In the late 1970s and early 1980s, Denver was also rumored to be the destination of various troubled franchises in both the National and American leagues, including the Chicago White Sox, Baltimore Orioles and Pittsburgh Pirates. Later, talk centered on the Minnesota Twins, Cleveland Indians and San Francisco Giants.

By the mid-1980s it was clear that acquiring an existing franchise would not be simple. The other option, gaining an expansion franchise, wouldn't be an easy matter either. Their noses bloodied by frequent player strikes and a successful challenge to the hallowed reserve clause (which bound a player to one team for life), major league owners were determined to avoid making hasty, ill-considered decisions concerning franchise shifts. More important, they were not about to give away valuable new franchises when they could command an exorbitantly high price for admission to their select club. Cities seeking new franchises had to offer state-of-the-art playing facilities, and local ownership groups had to make enormous up-front payments to the league.

Denver's successful campaign to bring major league baseball to Colorado has been well documented. What some optimists initially hoped could be achieved with a few friendly meetings and the stroke of a pen turned into an expensive, energy-draining, sometimes acrimonious ten-year struggle. The effort was marred by bankruptcies, ruined reputations, and seemingly endless disappointments. A hard-fought, narrowly successful vote on a new stadium bond issue and Denverites' enthusiastic commitments to season-ticket packages finally convinced the National League's Expansion Committee that the time was right and the city deserving. On July 5, 1991, Denver received the long-anticipated word that its bid had been accepted. The Colorado Rockies were officially born.

The birth had been difficult, and the team's early years promised more disappointments than triumphs. The Rockies' inaugural season of 1993 was a spectacular success in almost every respect except the won-lost column, although even there the team's 67–95 record set a new standard for success by a first-year franchise in the National League. Rockies pitchers were woefully ineffective, posting the league's worst earned run average, but the club featured some splendid hitters, including first baseman Andres "Big Cat" Galarraga, who won the league batting title with a career-high mark of .370. Dante Bichette and Charlie Hayes also provided notable power, and both batted over .300.

The 1994 season was somewhat of a letdown, largely because of the players' strike, which commenced on August 12 and canceled the remainder of the season, the league championship series, and the World Series. Yet most other indicators were positive. At the time of the strike, the Rockies appeared headed for a better record than that of the previous season, as their mark stood at 53–64. Several players were again enjoying banner seasons. Remarkably, attendance was almost 20,000 ahead of the total mark for the same number of games during the inaugural season, and club officials had hoped that the club would beat its own mark.

No attendance records will be established at Coors Field, the Rockies' new home. Even packed to capacity for every home game, the stadium could not host as many fans in a season as Mile High Stadium hosted during 1993. Some baseball purists were outraged that the Rockies christened the new stadium during the strike, using replacement players for a meaningless exhibition game on March 31, 1995. Their distress soon turned to joy, even rapture as the 1995 edition of the Rockies stayed at or near the top of the Western Division standings all season. Although the Los Angeles Dodgers barely nosed the Rockies out of the division title, the club clinched a berth in the National League playoffs in just its third season. No other expansion team had achieved such success so quickly. Although the 1996 club posted a winning record, it failed to reach the playoffs again, and some fans were disenchanted. However, as Coors Field ages gracefully and the Rockies win pennants and perhaps a World Series title or two in future decades, twenty-first-century baseball fans will have long forgotten such fleeting disappointments.

Courtesy JDenver Public Library, Western History Collection..

More than eighty years before Colorado finally fielded its major league team, regional fans avidly followed fortunes of other cities' teams in the big leagues. In this remarkable photograph, several thousand fans watch "live"action on a double-sided scoreboard set up in the Denver Auditorium Arena. The event is the 1911 World Series. Note that this audience is almost exclusively male. Far-sighted franchise owners were hard at work, seeking to make ball parks attractive for women and youngsters.

Courtesy Jay Sanford.

Smoky Joe Wood was one of the finest hurlers ever to appear on Colorado's sandlots. Born in Kansas City in 1889, he pitched in Ouray early in the twentieth century before graduating to the American Association in 1908. By the late summer of that year he was promoted to the Boston Red Sox, for whom he racked up 23 wins in 1911 and 34 in 1912.

Courtesy Jay Sanford.

Roy Hartzell was born and raised in Golden, where he died at age 80 in 1961. He enjoyed an eleven-year major league career between 1906 and 1916 with the St. Louis Browns and the New York High-landers (later renamed the Yankees) as an infielder, compiling a lifetime batting average of .252.

Courtesy Jay Sanford.

Bruno Konopka, pictured here with legendary manager Connie Mack, played briefly with the Philadelphia Athletics. He gained local fame as a star player for several teams in the *Denver Post* tournament during its heyday in the 1930s.

Courtesy Durango Heralk.

Excited fans greet the Colorado Rockies on the state's first major league opening day, April 9, 1993. To make the day complete, the Rockies crushed the Montreal Expos, 11-4, the first regular season win in the history of the franchise.

Courtesy Mark S. Foster.

The second official home opener at Coors Field, April 8, 1996. The Chicago Cubs and the Colorado Rockies are lined up for the National Anthem.

Courtesy Mark S. Foster..

Another view of opening day, 1996. Chicago Cubs' lead-off batter, Brian McRae, steps in as Rockies starter Kevin Ritz prepares to throw the first pitch of the 1996 home campaign.

SUGGESTED READINGS

Writer and sports fan George Plimpton observed back in 1982: "I have a theory—the larger the ball, the less writing about the sport. There are superb books about golf, very good books about baseball, not many books about football, and very few books about basketball. There are no books about beachballs." Baseball fans are fortunate to have many books from which to choose.

The standard works on baseball history are Harold Seymour, *Baseball* (Norman, 1960, 1971, 1990), and David Q. Voight, *American Baseball* (University Park, 1983 reprint). Geoffrey C. Ward and Ken Burns's *Baseball: An Illustrated History* (New York: 1994) is the companion volume to Burns's excellent PBS television series on baseball. Other more recent general histories include Charles Alexander, *Our Game: An American Baseball History* (New York, 1991), John Bowman and Joel Zoss, *Diamonds in the Rough: The Untold History of Baseball* (New York, 1989), Donald Honig, *Baseball: The Illustrated History of America's Game* (New York, 1990), and Benjamin G. Rader, *Baseball: A History of America's Game* (Urbana, 1992). Each one of these books has a bibliography that will point the reader to a host of other baseball-related readings. The various publications of the Society of American Baseball Research also hold a bonanza of articles on every aspect of baseball history.

Baseball has attracted interest from a wide range of authors about infinite topics. George F. Will's *Men at Work: The Craft of Baseball* (New York, 1990) provides superb insights into the game, and Roger Kahn's *The Boys of Summer* (New York, 1972), Jim Bouton's *Ball Four* (New York, 1970), Thomas Boswell's *Why Time Begins on Opening Day* (New York, 1984), and Roger Angell's *The Summer Game* (New York, 1962), *Five Seasons* (New York, 1978), and *Late Innings* (New York, 1982) have become classics. W. P. Kinsella's novel, *Shoeless Joe* (New York, 1982), captures the heart and soul of the game, as does the movie based on it, *Field of Dreams*.

Colorado baseball has not attracted that much attention but does offer a fascinating, if small, library of interesting books and articles. Two books to start with are Irvin Moss and Mark S. Foster, *Home Run in the Rockies: The History of Baseball in Colorado* (Denver, 1994), and Mark S. Foster, *The Denver Bears: From Sandlots to Sellouts* (Boulder, 1983). A special edition of *Colorado Heritage* (Spring 1995) is exclusively devoted to Colorado baseball. The arrival of the Rockies brought forth a host of articles and books on the team, including Allan Gottlieb, *In the Shadow of the Rockies: An Outsider's Look Inside a New Major League Baseball Team* (Niwot, 1994), and Bob Kravitz, *Mile High Madness: A Year with the Colorado Rockies* (New York, 1994). Duane A. Smith, "Baseball Champions of Colorado: The Leadville Blues of 1882," *Journal of Sports History* 4 (Spring 1977), takes a look at Colorado's greatest nineteenth-century team. General histories of Colorado, such as Carl Ubbelohde et al., *A Colorado History*, 7th edition (Boulder, 1995), place the game in the context of the state's history. For Denver the same may be said of Stephen J. Leonard and Thomas J. Noel, *Denver: Mining Camp to Metropolis* (Niwot, 1990).

There is hardly a town, county, or local history of Colorado that does not mention baseball as it was played by town teams well into the twentieth century. This was once the heart of the game. Two videos have been produced about Colorado baseball, "They Came to Play" (Denver KRMA-TV) and "Baseball Across the Great Divide" (Pueblo KTSC-TV). "Mile High Hopes: The Birth of the Rockies" is best for diehard Rockies fans.

These are just a few places to start looking at the captivating story of baseball in Colorado. Old local newspapers best recapture the flavor of the game and the times. Interviews of old-timers, old photographs, and even old baseball equipment also provide windows into games and players long gone.

INDEX

CPSIA information can be obtained at www.ICGtesting.com
Printed in the USA
LVOW051232180212

269324LV00001B/13/P

9 780870 814334